A LONG JOURNEY WALKED

A LONG JOURNEY WALKED

WITH GROWTH, LESSONS, AND ACHIEVEMENTS

MALINDI MTSWENI

PARTRIDGE

To order additional copies of this book, contact
Toll Free 800 101 2657 (Singapore)
Toll Free 1 800 81 7340 (Malaysia)
orders.singapore@partridgepublishing.com

www.partridgepublishing.com/singapore

Acknowledgment

I would like to acknowledge and thank everyone who contributed to the success of this book.

Big thanks to the Almighty God for giving me this magnificent wisdom and strength to be able to share my insight with the world. As a real unselfish leader I choose not to claim all the honour for the hard work and success of this book because without a collective effort from my team and their team spirit; the success and compilation of this book would not be possible.

- ➤ Partridge Singapore   : The Publishers
- ➤ Evelyn Keere-Mswetsa   : The editor
- ➤ Doctor Madolo-Mashele   : Script writer & Content Developer
- ➤ Ms Malindi Mtsweni   : Author

A vote of thanks to this following people

- Shongwe's family
- France Hlakudi
- Linah Malatjie

- Cherilee Alley
- Abram Masango
- Pastor Teddy and Nomsa Radebe
- All my Vitrovian team.

A big thanks to Partridge Singapore my publishers who made it a point that this book gets published so that my **Growth, Lessons and endless achievements** are shared with the world. My vision and my ideals about my country is exposed to the world.

Dedication

A long journey walked is dedicated to the fallen Queen that left no stones unturned!!! Lucy Majodina Mtsweni, born in 1952 and laid to rest on the 25 February 2017

You raised me up

The world and its desires pass away,
but whoever does the will of God lives forever.
1 John 2:17

In memory of Lucy, one of the top African National Congress Women's league (ANCWL) member; a worrier; a spear of the nation and a hero of all times within the South African. African National Congress (ANC), African National Congress Youth League (ANCYL) and African National Congress Women's league (ANCWL) has lost one of their legends. The society at large has lost a mother. She did what God intended her to do during her existence. She left a legacy for us to continue in-spite of life adversities. She walked a long journey with ***Growth, Lessons and Achievements***!!!

I choose not to mourn her forever now that she gave me all the knowledge to tackle life challenges as they come. Whist still alive she affirmed me that she will die peacefully because she saw me raising from nothing to something and taking good care of her, providing where I could. I am convinced that where ever where she is laid to rest, she is in peace.

I promise to carry her inspirational and wise words through the coming generations. Her total love and the spirit of Ubuntu (humanity) will always shine in my heart throughout my life.

I Malindi Mtsweni would love to say thank you mama for being a pillar of my strength in every situation of my life. Thanks for whispering in my ears in times of troubles reminding me that I am powerful beyond measure, when I felt weak and doubted my strength. I know that wherever you are, you are looking down upon me and are smiling with joy over the success that we both accumulated that is now benefiting the society at large.

Thank you Mama for the love you shared with me on earth may the Angels of God embraces you with love. Your seed has germinated into a tree that is now bearing the fruits that are enjoyed by everyone who comes into contact with me, Meme, your beloved daughter. Rest in harmony and let me run this race so as to better the future of the black race that has been rejected and isolated for so many years. Alluta continua!!! Better life for all.

TABLE OF CONTENTS

Acknowledgment v

Dedication vii

Introduction xi

Foreword xiii

Chapter 1   My Childhood And Life Lessons 1

Chapter 2   My Daughter Zinhle : The Ligth Of My Life.................8

Chapter 3   My Clear Cut Vision Of Success............................ 19

Chapter 4   Inviting God To Strengthen My Will Power 25

Chapter 5   The Birth Of Vitrovian 30

Chapter 6   The Wisdom Behind Proper Coordination Of Staff
            Members...43

Chapter 7   Sa Woman With The Ability
            To Run Their Own Race 48

Chapter 8   Lucky Ndinisa The Political Brain Engine Behind
            Malindi 57

Chapter 9   Let The Bygones Be Bygones................................63

Chapter 10 Gallery..68

Introduction

As I look at the world and the people living in it, I come to realize that every individual is greater than they think. All they need to do is to realize that. Some people were born to be like Eagles, they were meant to fly high but due reasons beyond their control, things like failed self-recognition; family background; unemployment and low self- esteem they behave like chickens. Chickens cannot fly and this may influence you if you are an eagle and you surround yourself with chickens. Your associates and surroundings can affect your mindset and daily routine such that as an eagle you will end-up believing that you can't fly.

I am a firm believer in the saying that goes: "it takes a Village to raise a child". I have a conviction that it is my duty, your duty and our duty to recognize the hidden potential in young South Africans and to assist them in unleashing the sleeping giant within themselves by reminding them over and over again that they are not chickens but eagles, and that they were naturally born to be free and to fly high till their goals and dreams are realized.

> *Through all the adversities of life I rose.*
> *Just like dust from the surface to the horizon I rose.*
> *I shone in the mist of the darkness to be the light for others.*

I swallowed my pride and invested my energy in helping the society at large.
I rose to do so willingly.
Just like a kite of success that rises against the wind of adversities I rose.
I chose to save the purpose of my existence on earth while I still could.
I chose not to sing: 'in my times', whilst I can still run the race to help the nation.
Obstacles and all life challenges knocked me down at times and continue to knock me down just like everyone else but I still rose.

As South Africans I urge all of us to practice the habit of doing more than we are paid for, going an extra mile!!! Great leaders understand and apply the principle of cooperative effort and are able to induce their followers to do the same. Leadership calls for power and power calls for cooperation.

Foreword

I am honoured with a privilege to introduce Alphonsinah Lindiwe Mtsweni's story to the world. This book is an amazing narrative that carries not only her dreams and aspirations, but many other African women who travelled similar paths that she took in her life. Undoubtedly, she had to go through trying times, crossing hurdles and obstacles along the way. As **Anatole France** puts it *"to accomplish great things we must not only act, but also dream, not only plan but also achieve"* and **Eleanor Rooseveld** further proclaimed: *"the future belongs to those who believe in the beauty of their dreams"*

Quite clearly, the love for her mom was so amazing and I admire her determination, dedication, self-discipline and diligence through which she drives her efforts in whatever she does, she literary does not wait for things to happen, she goes all out and make things happen. Her success is nothing more than a few disciplines practiced every day.

Alphonsinah Lindiwe Mtsweni affectionately known as "Meme", is indeed a prodigy who became my comrade, as we were secretaries, her being the secretary of the ANC Youth League (ANCYL) in the region and myself being her deputy secretary of the mother body. She also became my confidante, soulmate, and prayer-partner. One of her defining moments in her life, I recall, is when she was faced with very difficult challenges, and somehow through God's Grace, she emerged victorious and accepted Jesus Christ as her personal Saviour and became a gallant disciple of our Lord and Saviour. A celebrated author **Scott Peck** sums up this phenomenon: *"the truth is that our finest moments are most likely to occur when we are feeling deeply uncomfortable, unhappy or unfulfilled. For it is only in such moments, propelled by our discomfort that we are likely to step out of our ruts and start searching for different ways or true answers"*

I'm really blessed to be the one who ushers this lovely narrative to you all.

Take a leaf from this book and soldier on with your life journey.

Thank you

Mrs. Linah Masellane Malatjie
Executive Mayor: Nkangala District Municipality
3 August 2017

Chapter 1

My Childhood And Life Lessons

I, Alphonsinah Lindiwe Mtsweni AKA Malindi or Meme, was born on the 26th of August 1975 in the Highveld of Mpumalanga province presently known as Nkangala Region. This is the mining hub of Mpumalanga province in South Africa.

I was born in a family of few siblings, including my older brother by the name of Bhuti Mtsweni, from our loving and caring mother, Lucy Mtsweni, and my father, Zephania Mtsweni. My father was a contractor working day in and day out to assist my mom at home with all financial needs. In his spare time you find him building shacks houses (umjondolo) for the people around the area as a way of generating more income for us to survival. To me this stand as a symbol of taking responsibilities for those you love most.

We stayed in a shack with no electricity at Mtshali Street in a section called Vezi. I did my homework with a candle light because I had no excuses to my teacher for not doing my homework, and I really hated embarrassment. I was doing all of this because I was a goal-driven person working so hard to change my life and my family background.

I started my schooling at Sukumani Primary School and proceeded to Thuthukani Primary at Phola/Ogies around the 1980s. I was dedicated to my studies and very keen to reach high school, even though I did not come from a financially stable family.

Finally I graduated from primary school. This was sweet music to my ears, a real dream come true! I have always considered myself like everyone else, because we all have this belief that when you reach the high school level, then you are automatically closer to your dreams. So I had that feeling too. I started my high school at Mabande Comprehensive High School in the early 1990s. I really wanted to attend at this school because it was regarded as one of the best schools in the area. All facilities that one needed for one's studies were found there because it was a comprehensive high school. It had both theory and practise. It was fully equipped. This is where most boilermakers, welders, pipe-fitters, and motor mechanics were groomed.

Today when I look at the statistics of artisans that we have in our area, I feel so proud about all the teachers who played a role to those pupils' lives back then. As I think about all those teachers, I just smile from within. How could someone fail to make it in life when one was groomed by the likes of Mr Ndlovu, better known as Bhodloza, he was the headmaster of Mabande during those years. This man made it a point that when you wake up in the morning preparing to go to school, you first need to know the purpose of why you should go to school. Punctuality was his main principle, along with clean school uniforms and shining shoes. No student was above the others in his eyes; we were all treated the same, even when it came to punishment, corporal punishment was still considered legal at that time. As students, we all felt like we were abused.

But looking back to such treatment, one can simply say thanks to that traumatic treatment, because if it was not for that then, we wouldn't have reached this far. By so saying, I'm not condoning corporal punishment but merely saying it made us what we are and who we are today. Majority of the learners who attended school with me during those years have made it in life.

Congress of South African students (COSAS) was introduced to our school and I was in the forefront with the likes of Liver Lubisi, Vusi (Veti), Mandla Mngomezulu. I served as one of the school representative council (SRC) members. My duty was:

- to help organise learners through democratically elected SRCs ·
- to encourage students to serve the community, remind them that we are members of society before we are students and thereby showing that students can play a progressive role in the broad democratic alliance.
- to show them that in serving the community, they are playing a role in the overall struggle of the people of South Africa.
- to create awareness that the duty of the students was to lend support to trade unions and community organizations.

I decided to change schools and went to a new school which was a bit distant from home but was in the same location just different sections. The distance did not matter at all.

I was so glad at Mehlwana High school due to the fact that my position as an SRC member was still recognized and I was given a platform to deal with student issues and my studies were not affected. So I did what I do best fighting for the rights of all students.

It was at Mehlwana High school were I completed my matric. My mother budgeted for me to go a matric farewell function but i chose to take that money and bought clothes for my siblings. I then went from one department to another working so as to gain experience.

I grew up with all these dominating thoughts in my mind; questions with no answers.

Highveld has all types of power stations and factories for manufacturing and productions; however unemployed rate for youth is still high. Surely something must be done for our province.

As I look around the place where I was born and raised as a child, my teenage years, I feel so fortunate. Mpumalanga Province was blessed with a girl child and is still blessed. Going up the Mpumalanga map, at the Lowveld, there is a town known as Mbombela, you will find all the riches that agriculture can produce. Mbombela is a tourist attraction, one of the best places in South Africa to spend your vacation at. Game lodges and beautiful resorts are found in the middle of a tropical forest, between the mountains. This is the place where tourists get an opportunity to have a full view of all the wild animals, including the 'Big Five' as they tour.

When you touch base on farming, you simply know that production and exporting is what creates job opportunities for the residents and give a boost to the economy. The sad part about all of this is that when you look at the statistics of the unemployed youth within the region, you start to wonder.

I spent my quality time day by day trying to figure out all the answers and solutions towards this matter, but answers were nowhere to be found. Deep down in my heart, I knew that something is needed to be done to change this situation.

Lucy Mtsweni, my mom, shared with me how difficult it was to raise us as a domestic worker while my father was doing some odd jobs at any construction site available, just to put food on the table for all of us.

She would say: "As I compared our basic salaries, I earned better than him, however we were pulling together in the same direction. We made sure that we both brought food home. We were both doing this for the best interest of our kids. Along the way, my husband decided to take a different direction and I was left alone with all of my kids. I didn't know what to do. I was heartbroken, and tried so hard to hide it from my children, however you, Meme, you noticed that and became closer to me for comfort and security.

We carried on with life through prayer. Each and everything that I used to get from where I was working I took home.

One day the cops came to my workplace and told me that my house had burnt to the ground. I couldn't believe it until I reached home, and surely there was no house anymore. Everything was in ashes. I just fell down to the ground and became tight-lipped; I could not say a word.

My kids were standing right behind me, in their school uniforms because this incident took place whilst still at school. They were all in shock. The school uniform that they were wearing was the only clothes they had.

I expected my family members from my husband's side to come and give support now that they were informed about the situation, but no one came nor provided a helping hand. My family was far away; most of them resided in the Free State. At that stage, I came to believe that when days are dark, everyone shies away from you. I was supported by the community I stayed amongst.

They donated everything they could, including blankets, clothes and food. We were squeezed into some rooms just to sleep for a night. I didn't give up, and I never looked back, because I was already faced with other challenges. This whole situation made me not to be fastidious when it came to job opportunities. Every bitter thing had to taste sweet, now that I was hungry with my kids. Life threw lemons at me and I made lemonade.

I continued to work and built a one-room shack just for my kids and me to have a place to sleep. There was no privacy at all. And no one was worried about that because our main objective was to have a shelter over our heads."

I was doing well at school, but the biggest challenge was my school uniform. I never had a complete school uniform. Sometimes I had no school shoes, when I got them, the jersey will be torn and when I get the jersey the skirt or shirt will be worn-out. Even paying the school fees was a challenge at times. My mother would go to Mr. Nyathikazi, at Mabande High School, and negotiate for our school fees; it was me, Bhuti, Mavu and Bafana. By the grace of the Lord, they allowed me to carry on with my studies. I was grateful about it because I knew that one day I will change my life for the better. My mother was constantly praying for me to pass at school.

In my life experience I came to believe that God will never forsake His people in times of trouble because even though I felt deserted by my relatives, the Shongwe's family filled that gap. They did everything they could to assist us. They paid our school fees and bought us school uniform. They became our extended family in everything that we couldn't afford they were always there to give a helping hand. On the 16th June 1989, Phola township community members decided to fight against the bucket toilet system. A toilet system that was unhygienic, the upraising was a demand for proper sanitation. A protest march was organised. I was in the forefront with Thokozani AKA Botoboto. The march was directed to the municipal offices demanding proper service delivery. It was an innocent violent free march because we were not armed. Our biggest sin was to sing revolutionary songs and we never saw it coming, in no time the police were all over us. They shot Thokozani very badly in front of me. I tried all i could to save his life by applying all the first-aid skills i knew until the paramedics arrived and took him to Hendrick Verwoerd hospital in Pretoria which is now known as Steve Bantu Biko academy.

I supported his family in every step of the way even though I was still young at that time. He spent six months in hospital because of serious injuries suffered. I took it upon myself to be the witness against the case that was opened against the state. He later passed away however it was due to natural causes, may his soul rest in peace.

All these took place because of the total love that I have for the liberation our people and for the good quality service delivery that they deserve to get.

"Do not judge me by my successes,
Judge me by how many times I
Fell down and got back up again."
- Nelson Mandela

That is how a politician, philanthropist and businesswoman in me was evoked, enhanced, developed and came to be.

Chapter 2

My Daughter Zinhle : The Ligth Of My Life

Giving birth to my first born child made me realise the real reason for my existence.

I asked myself a number of questions, I was worried and was wondering about my future and her future in this world. Raising her was not a big challenge at all because I had my family as a support structure.

My main worry was about what is transpiring in the world today, drug abuse; crime; discrimination and all other social-ills. As parents we all believe that we are in full control of our kids. We believe that they will choose right as they grow. We try hard to protect them from being swallowed or consumed by the negativity that this world has to offer.

We work very hard daily trying to plant new seeds in to their minds. Seeds that will grow into trees, trees that will produce fruits, not bitter fruits but fruits that can be enjoyed by everyone.

Upon the arrival of Zinhle on earth, I then knew there and then that my battle has begun. I had to eliminate some of the things in my life, cut off and made some adjustments to all the things that would hinder my being a good mother. This was not only for my child however for every child in my community.

I regard my daughter as the light of my life because through her and because of her birth my entire life was transformed. I started compiling the kind of freedoms I would like for her.

The kind of freedoms I wished for my daughter

- *I wanted my child to worship at any church of her choice.*
- *I wanted her to choose her own friends (and I will just give advice)*
- *I wanted her to attend at any school or tertiary institution of her choice.*
- *I wanted her to choose her own studies and career.*
- *I wanted her to be married in a race/tribe of her choice.*
- *I wanted her to participate in any sports activities of her choice.*
- *I will assist her to discover her hidden talent and give support to pursue it.*
- *I also wanted her to enjoy the freedom of being a born free generation more than anything else.*

As I finished compiling this kind of freedoms for Zinhle something crossed my mind and touched my soul. I was in tears when I started to realize that there are a number of kids on South African streets who are homeless because they were abandoned by their parents.

When you talk about parental love to them it is like something new to their ears because they were never exposed to it, they don't even know how it feels like to be loved by your own parents. That is the reason they are found everywhere just like autumn leaves because they don't know where they belong, they just go to any direction the wind sends you, from east to south, from north to west.

This is very touching particularly when you pay attention to it and has a full view to what is happening to South African abandoned children today. It pains me because nowadays drug smugglers takes them from the streets and uses them as drug mules use them for prostitution and to commit crime for them.

In spite of all this as a parent I sat down and compiled a plan for the future of my daughter amidst all the fears and doubts that this life has to offer.

This confirmed to me that i have to play a required role to save the nation. As I wipe my tears off I realized that Zinhle is so fortunate to have me as a mother, who is prepared to lead her through the ups and downs of life.

As we all know that we are all visitors or passersby' in this world, I spend most of my time sharing and giving her all the necessary information in preparation for the day I will be no more.

Oh! Yes I must say it is very interesting to have a daughter who has qualities and character traits that are more similar like yours, someone that you can laugh with and cry with, your own mirror image, a true reflection of what you are, that's Zinhle to me.

As parents I think we should try hard to act likewise, encouraging our children to familiarize themselves with libraries because that's where the hidden treasure of success of this world is found. This is a plea to every parent because I personally discovered that through reading there is light because one gets empowered, your grammar, vocabulary and knowledge improves. There are a number of books that one can make his/her own collection from.

These are some of the books which formed part of my collection and I live by its principles:

- The law of success or Think and grow rich: Author- Napoleon HILL.
- Advance your life: Author- Dr John Tibane.
- Leadership 2020: Author- Sibusiso Leope (DJ SBU)
- Capitalist Nigger: Author- Chika Onyeani.
- Take charge in times of challenge: Author- Dr David Molapo.
- Exposing a hidden giant: Author- Ben Gumede

The knowledge and wisdom that is found in these books is not only meant to empower the youth but for every individual from all different walks of life. Remember you might believe that your knowledge is enough based on your academic achievements until you start reading such books, that's when you will realize that what you know is not enough.

I did not only invest in transferring knowledge, wisdom and all that i know to my daughter, I also took out some insurance policies for her so that she can be covered financially. I work hard to secure her future. However there is nothing that beats spending quality time with your kids.

Zinhle is my first born child the first and the last, none in between. I have leant to be her best friend because it broke my heart to see her in the house playing and even doing house chores all by herself. At first it was difficult to come to her level but with time i became good at it. When we travel together in the car I listen to her type of music and even use her type of language, the slang. I have seen her smiling very wide and even becoming happy when I use slang and the youthful jargon. This is how we plant seeds of remembrance straight into their hearts; whilst still alive by investing all our love. Trust me this does not even cost a rand or a single dollar. Remember good things are for free!!!

One of my principles which I wish my daughter to continue when I am no-more is that of children who suffer at the hand of step parents. This problem is normally ignored by many. In most cases those kids are forced to pretend to be ok whilst inside they are in tartars. These kids looks like ordinary kids and normal however i have seen them traumatised and abused and this destroying them. There is a great element of abuse taking place behind closed doors. Some parents choose to ignore their kids and turn a blind eye to the signs of abuse. These kids are exposed to psychological and emotional trauma that makes most of our young South Africans to go astray.

They end up developing a self-hatred in such a way that they can't even share any love with the next person because they never experienced love.

Most of them become demoralized in their activities and even about life itself. So I Malindi Mtsweni I personally choose to blow the whistle and break the silence because silence is not always golden. I plan on bringing together the department of social development, psychologists and the spiritual care givers and come up with solutions to this problem in particular.

We can have a number of workshops around the country dealing with this matter and make a difference. This can be documented in a manual or a guide to parents who find themselves in a situation where they have to be step parents.

My wish is for me to emulate people who makes a difference, defend democracy and wants to see better lives for all. I am talking about the likes of …

- Nelson Rolihlahla Mandela
- Mahatma Ghandi
- Steve Bantu Biko
- Linda Corby

I am saying this with a heavy heart torn into pieces, especially when I think of how Zinhle was raised. Every time I look at her I simply say "she's the rose that grows in a concrete crack".

She grew up in a one room shack with my mother and my younger brother Keme while I was at work trying to make ends meet. I was working as a casual at Matla coal. I got terrified every time I paid a visit at home to check on my daughter. The environment under which my daughter was living disheartened me. My mom had to always create a small fire place inside the house just to make sure that it is always warm in the house for Zinhle. It was winter and very cold and when the fire goes off, she cried and my mom will quickly awake and prepare another fire assisted by Keme. I decide to work on my budget and extended the house to be a 3 roomed house working hand in hand with my mom. My life started to change for good and Zinhle was now safe and secure with all the things that a child could ever need to grow well.

It was during that time when I was elected as a ward councillor, and things started shaping up for the better. I never looked back.

Zinhle's testimony: "As the one and only lovely daughter of Malindi I still look up to the sky trying to understand this blessing that God gave me. Having such a wonderful mom in life is truly a blessing. She is more of a mentor in my life, a one on one guidance type of a parent. A mother that doesn't just talk but does practical things that you can learn from her or follow in her footsteps.

The amazing part of my life that I like most is that I am a witness on how difficult it was for her to start all what she has accumulated today. Life was not easy at all for her back then not only for her but for our family at large but she stood tall and decided to transform that bitter life to this current better life that we have today.

The empire that she had built has changed and touched so many lives. If it might happen that she dies tomorrow I will break down and cry with a devastated heart that is broken into pieces but with one thing in mind that she may be gone but never be forgotten and all her teachings remain within me forever.

One of her best teachings is, the art of giving this has become a norm in our family. This type of generosity was transferred by my granny Lucy to my Mom and my mother transferred it to me and to the rest of the family. I strongly believe that the seed planted in our lives will be transferred from one generation to another generation. We strongly believe that blessed are the hands that give more than the one that receives. This goes with a total understanding of knowing that I am that I am because of your existence around me, for one to feel his or her human nature needs other people around him.

"You have not lived today until you have done something for someone who can never repay you. We cannot build our own future without helping others to build theirs". By: Bill Clinton.

Thank You Mom

To be a mother who has to raise kids by herself is not an easy task to do

Yet you do it proudly everyday no matter what life offers you to do.

You have groomed, natured and turned me, your baby into a beautiful young lady in the universe.

You were there for me since the very beginning and saved me countless tears crying even though at times there was no reason to cry.

As I grow older being doomed and blind folded by the bitterness and the peer pressure of this world,

You decided to give the pushy and wise advice to carry me through the years.

With my every mistake or wrongful deed,

you were always there to understand and call me in to order.

You put no limits on my dreams or anything else I wish to do.

You never forget to say you care or how much you love me.

The smile and tears upon your face when I achieve, when I listen to your advice and follow on your footsteps provides me with more value in my heart than you'd ever imagine.

There is no other person that will shape my heart the way you've done,

your job is finished perfectly on your precious daughter that I am today, your true reflection, your physical mirror of all the years.

I imaged silence in my lonely room thinking that if you were not there for me what could I have become? In this days and age of the world dominated with drugs and the spread of HIV & Aids.

There was never a single moment of time of not having you by my side because you chose to walk with me and teach me how to fly.

You are a wonderful mother to die for.

You have always put me first with your total love and my whole life is not enough time for me to repay you.

I always put my disagreements aside and manage to make it through.

I know that my teen years have driven you crazy but you have guided me with assurance all the way.

You have given me comfort and certainty with every breath I take within the day.

Your little girl is growing up but your baby girl will always remain deep inside me.

There are not enough words that can thank you for everything; you have helped me emotionally and physically. Through you I've learn not to feel embarrassed by my failures but to learn from them and start again.

I have my whole future ahead of me and you are the women that has led me and guided me towards the proper path.

How can one simple day prove that much thanks and love to someone who has pushed this far and still is working her way?

No other person deserves to be loved more than you Mom.

Thanks for transforming such love to me Mom and I promise that I will carry it through and also transform it to my family when I get married one day.

- By: Zinhle

Having two people who dearly love you and always ready to protect you through all the adversities of life is just a blessing. My granny and my mom are just two combined element of my life. They are like the left eye while the other one is the right eye, as to see where I could not see.

God will really punish me if I fail to say thanks to Him for having given me amazing parents. Remember most of my peers are faced with lots of family emotional distress due to the disputes within families. These are some of the contributory factors that make most scholars to fail to concentrate on their careers. Anyone can testify that there is no better place for a human being than home.

A home with family members that are united provides stability, peace, love and a sense of belonging. I am what I am because I belong somewhere and this helps me to dream bigger about my career.

Looking at the love that I have for fashion it makes me always dream about the fashion empire that I wish to establish and create job opportunities for the people. I need to start my own clothing label, a brand that will be accommodative to every individual from different walks of life.

My company will manufacture everything in doors from shoes, hand bags, luggage bags, cloths, belts and also find a way of associating my brand with its own cosmetics (body lotion, soap, body spray, roll on and shower gel). If it happens that my mom wish me to form part of Vitrovian as I am about to complete my studies at university, I will be happy to be one of the Vitrovian staff members. I will do all the internal duties like every employee and follow all the instructions and the code of conduct of the company but not forgetting to establish my own clothing factory as I go along.

This factory will be the brain child of Vitrovian because Vitrovian is where everything starts, where all our dreams are made and becomes a reality.

What I like most about my mom is that she does not have a rubbish bin for her employees, no employee is a reject in her face maybe the reason behind this motive is that she's was once rejected and been thrown in a rubbish bin by people who denied to give her the opportunity to establish Vitrovian.

They threw her away, closing all doors for her vision, dreams and goals; therefore she doesn't want anybody to be in the same kind of situation because she has been there, down there, experiencing all those pains.

Remember my mom when she gives you a job she knows it for a fact that she is not only saving your life but your family as well. Surely there is no rubbish bin for human beings.

Remember that the builder's rejected stone might become a chief Conner stone of the house, so be wise reject no one in life because for that particular person to exist it means there's a role to be played, He might be a missing link. Every time you think that you have been rejected, just stick to your guns because you might be actually being re-directed to something better.

My mom taught me that in life I need not to be like most people who uses their qualifications and think they will do the job, but rather do a perfect task on hand and then the Diploma will come as a back up to compliment my excellent work.

"Success does not consist in never making blunders, but in never making the same mistake the second time around." by **Linda Corby**

That is how a daughter, woman, and a Mother in me was motivated, encouraged, developed and came to be.

Chapter 3

My Clear Cut Vision Of Success

A vision to my understanding is a mental picture of your desired future.

It is a mental picture of where you would like to see yourself, your business, your school or organization, in the future. If you have a dream in life it is a matter of protecting that dream and if you want something then go get it because time wasted will never be regained.

When I was a regional secretary for ANCYL in Nkangala I worked with Linah Malatjie who happened to be an ANC Regional deputy Secretary. Linah became a sister to me, she groomed me, and she taught me lots of things about life. Our relationship became so strong such that I started to regard her as my mother. She played a significant role in my life, she was my mentor.

She then arranged a computer studies for the both of us. She encouraged me to capacitate myself. She paid for all the short courses we attended. Together we passed, we made it, and from that experience I learnt that

All the fees for those short courses were arranged and paid by her. We then stood together and pass the course. In a nutshell these small achievements really boosted our self-esteem and also encouraged us to keep moving forward and study more and more.

Most people in life are told that they will never make it in life; it is these words that should push you and not break you down, prove them wrong, because the enemy is within, what you think about yourself is more powerful than what the world think about you. Frustration is caused by trying to hit a target that you cannot see.

Whenever I converse with people on a daily basis, I have discovered that majority of the people are not aware that family and friends are the dream or vision and passion killers. It has become evident to me that many people who have no direction and no vision wakes up every day and try to talk others out of their dreams and things they are passionate about as a way of demoralizing them. Remember these are the people that you mostly expect them to give you support but trust me, when I say you stand a lesser chance to get support from them.

You can choose your friends but cannot choose your family, and by so saying I do not mean any harm, offence or any form of insult: I am mentioning this because I have met so many people whose dreams were crashed by those who are close to their hearts. So be warned and be very alert about who you share your dreams with, rather keep everything in your journal till the day you put your dream into practice. Learn to protect your dream. Look for the right people; projects; companies that could help your dreams to become reality. In the book of Proverbs 29:18, it says: "Where there is no vision, the people perish."

When you don't have a vision, you will end up working for someone who has a vision and you will make their vision become a reality at the expense of your happiness. So live your dream, create your own reality by choosing your future. It is necessary to work on yourself and develop yourself every day.

VICTORY requires payment in advance"

Allow Yourself

Allow yourself to dream,
And when you do dream big

Allow yourself to learn
And when you do learn all you can

Allow yourself to laugh
And when you do share your laughter

Allow yourself to set goals
And when you do reward yourself as you move forward
                                    by Catherine Pulsifer 2009

When you don't have a vision, you struggle to get out of bed and give those blankets a kick, because you have no goal to chase. You sleep with no plan for tomorrow. I saw many people drown in front of me because there is nothing exciting to look forward to. Instead of making the day count, instead of seizing each and every single moment, they found themselves trapped, frustrated, in bed and broke! They lack passion and drive in their lives.

When you do not have a vision, you waste the potential, gift, and skills that the Almighty has given you. God gave you the potential to be great. You were created by the most creative Creator so therefore you will always remain a creative creature. So what are you waiting for, just make that move. Your reward to God is how you use the potential, gift and skills He gave you.

When you do not have vision, you start envying people with a vision and want to imitate them. Choose not to be a follower; choose not to be a spectator ; because you will end up like most people who are visionless whose mission is to look for ways to bring down those who visionary.

When you do not have a vision, you focus on what you do not want, rather than what you want. You will do things just to earn a living rather than what you are passionate about.

I saw many people who decided to choose careers which they were not meant for, careers they don't love or are not passionate about, and for all the wrong reasons for instance, money or popularity; three (3) months down the line they are discouraged and become unproductive. A person may be a doctor by profession but an Artist in heart a singer by birth. So it is very wise to do soul searching before you make a decision.

Do what you love and love what you do. In Dr John Tibane's book, "Enlightened Leadership", he says: "Focus is essential, because whatever we focus on expands, focusing on the problems of the present makes our problems bigger than they are, and we become intimidated; focusing on the possibilities of the future makes our possibilities of success bigger, and we become inspired."

Nelson Mandela once shared this quote: "Our deepest fear is not that we are inadequate, our deepest fear is that we are powerful beyond measure. We ask ourselves who am I to be brilliant, gorgeous, talented and fabulous. Actually who are you not to be? We were born to manifest the glory of God that is within us. And as we let our own light shine, we are unconsciously giving other people a permission to do the same".

In a nutshell this is more about being afraid of being yourself, a king; an entrepreneur; a leader or an icon because you are afraid of being yourself not what the world will say about you or think about you.

It takes people a long time to answer a simple question:" What do you want in life"?

They are very quick to respond about the things that they don't want in life. So people find themselves focusing on what they do not want in life rather than what they want and they end up getting what they do not want because where the focus is, energy follows and magic happens.

If you do not focus on what you want, what you don't want will soon take over and you will be doomed in the middle of no were. As the saying goes behind a successful man there is a strong woman (to give guidance and direction). So in my case it was difficult because I am a woman who is aiming to rise against all odds.

Then who is that man that was supposed to be there to give me guidance and direction, meaning? I had to run the race by myself. I am the greatest that is why I am where I am today.

Important things to remember when creating a vision:

o   Know exactly who you are.
o   Brainstorm, imagine and dream.
o   Focus on things that give your life purpose and meaning.
o   Do not put limits to your dreams.
o   A total believe is required in everything you do.
o   Have morals so that you can be able to associate easily with others.
o   Have purpose for life.
o   The need to change, know why you should change your life.
o   The basic success concept is needed.
o   Be the action program kind of a person.
o   Write down your goals because that will create a sense of purpose
o   Remember life without meaningful goals creates nothing but frustrating emptiness
o   Do not react to every challenge evaluate first
o   Spend too much time in your life developing your mind.
o   Use the knowledge you have constructively and positively
o   Learn to balance the following in your life: spiritual, mental, financial, family and social.

As a reader and an author from Helen Keller I have learnt that the most pathetic person in the world is someone who has sight, but has no vision.

I had a clear cut vision about my destiny.

What I Want

I have made the choices. I have held the thoughts.
I have taken the actions to create my current reality.
And I have the power to change it into whatever I want
it to be.

With the choices I make, I am constantly fulfilling the
vision I have for my life.

If that does not seem to be the case -
Then I am deceiving myself about what I really want.
Because what I really, truly want, I will get!

What I truly wanted in the past, I already have.

Poet: Unknown

"The best way to predict the future is to create it."
- Peter Drecker

*That is how a motivator, a visionary, and a go-getter in me was
motivated, encouraged, developed and came to be.*

Chapter 4

Inviting God To Strengthen My Will Power

I was born in a family that believes in God, from my early years of Sunday school till today.

I still invite God to give direction. My mother gave me something that money can never buy that is the word of God. This is one of the things that make me to always look back and smile back to the world and just say thanks Mama for raising me under the wings and the wisdom of God.

As a child I did not understand the main purpose of being close to God but now I know that God is the only answer. I wanted to start a business that will not only benefit me but the society at large, not for my family and relatives but the entire community, a company that will alleviate poverty and bring back the moral understanding of oneself irrespective of family background.

Remember God gave us the guts to be great, to be the best and to win against all odds. No matter how big my dream was, I had no fear due to the fact that God was on my side. I was carried over by this dominating believe that says God will never forsake me. Starting my own company was going to expose me to a number of things which will only need God's intervention and God's power, nothing else or even nobody.

> "When you are going through something hard
> and wonder where GOD is,
> Remember, the teacher is always quiet during a test."

I knew it deep down in my heart that God will help me lead everyone with respect and with dignity. I was doing all this because I never wanted to be like most leaders who put profit first and the people driving the business last.

People who spend their time making sure that they deliver the best and make things happen. I wanted to be a leader that put herself in her employees shoes and feel what they are feeling and assist them were I could. This goes with how I was raised and the dominating spirit of *ubuntu* within me. I think through poverty I have learnt to understand myself and the people around me better. One once told me that in life you need to learn to entertain everyone you meet do not ignore strangers because at times you might be ignoring an angel speaking to you face to face because God use other people to deliver a massage.

I grew up attending Zionist church with my whole family. The church dress code was a proof as to how serious and how proud we are of our church and belief. The neatness of the church uniforms was a sign of the congregation respecting God.

As I grew older I then started to have a freedom of choice, this was not based on comparing churches with their class but just having a complete freedom of choice. I then started attending at Assemble church of Christ and now I am at the Light house prophetic ministry church. I can proudly say I have grown a lot spiritually, from where I started to where I am now.

I came to understand that when God speaks He doesn't give you solutions that make sense to you at times but He only expect you to have faith and trust that things will get better. Every day of our lives we get tested by tricky situations where we have to make decisions or choose a side. It is at times like these that we need to listen to our inner self and use the wisdom that God gave us. If God was not in my life I think I could have perished long time ago. I would not be where I am today with all this wisdom.

Wiser people have said if you know better then you will do better, so for me to know better about the good things that God does to His people. I think that is the reason I still do better in life even today.

Trials and Temptations

Consider it pure joy, my brothers and sisters, whenever you face trials of any kind, because you know that the testing of your faith produces perseverance. Let perseverance finish its work so that you may mature and complete, not lacking anything. If any of you lacks wisdom, you should ask God, who gives generously to all without finding fault, and it will be given to you, however when you ask, you must believe and not doubt, because the one who doubts is like a wave of the sea, blown and tossed by the wind.

The presence of God is imperceptible but those who really pray hard they can tell you that when He is around you can feel His presence without being told. My advice is the next time you think God is talking to you, kneel down and pray about it, your answers will come.

I have been through tragedies in life but through the wisdom of God I did manage to turn that tragedy into strategy, my pains into passion and my confusion into courage. When they say God never fails, they really mean it He doesn't fail at all. I can testify. On my journey to open my company (Vitrovian) as a chair woman God provided me with all the strength to achieve my dream. His glory was upon me and to everyone who supported me. I therefore said OH!! Lord my God, you are my redeemer saying this with a smile and the tears of joy.

Know that it is done

Every prayer is answered and grace is always given. If you fear that your prayer will not be answered, then ask for help in understanding and seeing your answered prayer more clearly. Trust that you will see the love in every answered prayer. You are known completely and loved unconditionally by the Angels. Nothing that will serve you is ever withheld from you.

Ask for help

Angels offers us 24/7 help; the more receptive we are, the more help we get. If you diminish your receptivity, you limit the Angels' ability to help you. Create your own invocations, or prayers, that specifically call for the help you need. Realize that when you call upon an Angel, what really happens is that you open yourself to greater receptivity to their assistance.

Listening and Doing

My dear brothers and sisters, take note of this: Everyone should be quick to listen, slow to speak and slow to become angry, because human anger does not produce the righteousness that God desires. Therefore, get rid of all moral filthiness and the evil that is so prevalent and humbly accept the word planted in you, which can save you.

Do not merely listen to the word, and so deceive yourselves, do what the word says. Anyone who listens to the word but does not do what it says is like someone who looks at his face in a mirror and, after looking at himself, goes away and immediately forgets what he looks like, whoever that looks intently into the perfect law that gives freedom, and continues in it, not forgetting what they have heard, but doing it, they will be blessed in what they do.

Those who consider themselves religious and yet do not keep a tight rein on their tongues deceive themselves, and their religion is worthless. Religion that God our Father accepts as pure and faultless is this: to look after orphans and widows in their distress and to keep oneself from being polluted by the world.

Humble your selves before God and you shall receive.

My favourite scriptural quote is
"Be still and know that I am God" Psalms 46 verse 10

Dr Bill Winston once said "Your feet will never take you where your mind has never been".

That is how a prayer warrior, a humble soul, and a doer of the word in me was motivated, encouraged, developed and came to be.

Chapter 5

The Birth Of Vitrovian

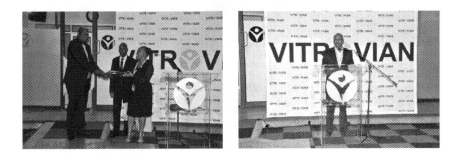

Vitrovian is one of the best initiatives that I have ever achieved in my life. This is a company that really makes me proud, due to the impact that it has made in the society. It has touched so many lives and will continue to impact on many lives in years to come.

Starting this business was not easy at all. There were lot of challenges that gave me sleepless nights. I was struggling to get a place where I can locate and position my ideal business. I was rejected by those who had the authority to sign all the required documentation. I was sent from pillar to post day by day up until I realized that they are refusing to give me the platform of hiring their vacant offices in town. I think in this case their refusal was motivated by gender and race.

I must say the idea behind Vitrovian was really posing a threat to some of the existing companies. All this did not stop me to pursue my dream. I kept fighting and pushing with a clear understanding behind the word *push* (persist until something happens).

I finally got to rent a building at Save-Way shopping complex where my new 'baby' was born. I was now feeling the presence of God in my life. Remember I have mentioned that I needed God to strengthen my will power. As I was raised in a Christian family I was taught to put God first in everything I do.

Oh!! Yes I must rephrase and re-emphasize, I was denied an opportunity to start Vitrovian but because of the fact that God is a God of all miracles and no darkness shall overcome His willingness, so I made it.

My first car that was used for the business was a simple Ford Bantam. All the office materials that were needed this small car was able to carry everything for the- business to run.

The key role players that made Vitrovian to be up and running are Norman Mogapi better known as (uSomahashi) the provider of all time and my right- hand wing in most of the decisions I made.

Pheli Mogapi, Simon Motshweni, Emmanuel Mashego AKA "KG the Conversationalist, and Sunday Mathebula and these became the management team which is headed by my good self. They are very dedicated, loyal, professionals and have the spirit of *ubuntu* that made our company to grow bigger and faster.

I would also like to give honour to my staff members who were not only coming to work to make money but to give their all so that Vitrovian can grow bigger and stronger. I am talking about the likes of Kate Radebe, Prudence Msiza, Nathi Lukhele, Daniel Lubisi, Gladness Ubisi, Ntombi Sibande, Bongani Lukhele, Edwin Maisela, Linda Zwane, Precious Tshukudu and Ezekiel Mogapi. Every time when I look back I come to notice that it takes a dedicated team to achieve a vision. Without all these people mentioned above my company was not going to be what it is today.

To be honest our offices had no furniture at first for some few months and some of my staff members were starting to be demoralized due to the fact that the payment was delaying from Eskom (Kusile), our major supporting partner. Some were starting to lose hope but they never reached a point of quitting the company because they were driven by the growth of the company more than anything else, and I still respect them for being so brave and being so loyal to the vision of this company.

As a woman of the struggle I was supported by other women, for me, Malindi to be where I am today I know for a fact that the women charter played a crucial role to pave my way so as to achieve the best in life.

Abram Masango, Kusile Power station Project Director then now Acting CEO of Eskom Enterprises and subsidiaries tells more about how Vitrovian was born and why.

Vitrovian as a community liaison company for Kusile was a stepping stone to our way of working on improving links and communicating with our immediate communities. We had to establish honest, open and very humble relations with business chambers, community leaders and people from various townships and districts.

To be able to deal with issues of communities easily, we needed to appoint a company that specifically handled that on behalf of the project or the business.

This concept is most often misunderstood by a lot of business leaders. It is important for the community to hear a voice that they trust. A voice and the face they know have their best interest at heart. An individual trusted by both the business and the community.

It is not easy for communities to trust companies and it is equally important for businesses to respect this reality about communities. This is why we established ties that govern and synchronize communications, monitors plans, requests and important initiatives that build and empower communities.

The Eskom Kusile Project had more than 120 companies on site that faced a communication challenge in regards to communicating with employees from the various feeder areas and areas around the district of Nkangala interns of recruitment, corporate social investment and social development. The Projects efforts, reputation and image were not managed as well as not being favorably positioned in the minds of the external stakeholder.

Vitrovian was identified as the most appropriate vehicle to provide a solution by becoming a communication bridge between the community and the Eskom Project site.

This led to the successful implementation of corporate social investment in the region with sustainable and suitable initiatives and projects' being successfully executed. This increase in spending by companies towards the greater good to the tune of 120 million Rands towards communities was unprecedented.

Other attempts to accomplish the same results had failed dismally; these included the distribution of information using the Apartheid method of dropping flyers using a helicopter in the respective communities. A method that was inappropriate and led to community uprisings targeted at the project, leading to project instability.

Vitrovian became the most effective organisation that successfully identifies and implements Corporate Social Investment, Social Development, Co- operatives, Recruitment and Project Stability. Truly Vitrovian became a community facilitator and developer.

Vitrovian did this very well, assisting the project. Vitrovian is a group of young people who understands the language and the needs of the youth in their own communities. Some of them were former young leaders and politicians so they knew how to best tackle some of the challenges the majority of communities had, in an honest and efficient way.

They could relate to some of these concerns. From that point of view, when I look at where we are with our social standing, I am convinced that we made our mark in empowering our people and continue to construct, whilst walking the journey with them. I am sure in this noble pursuit we have not forgotten our mandate to South Africa and the continent at large.

The parliament portfolio committee that has made several visits to our projects gave us confidence as they applauded some of the systems we have put in place. They also commended the manner in which Kusile drives certain aspects and its involvement with the communities over the years.

In a mega project like Kusile, one cannot say the system that one puts in place today, is relevant tomorrow. It is important to keep sharpening the pencil all the time.

Things change constantly in every dynamic environment and that keeps me on my toes. Simple things can have real effect on people. For example dealing with a community that has a new leader might require a modified approach. So from time to time we need to find the best mechanisms that can best suit the situation at hand.

As part of pushing the agenda in terms of local beneficiation and localization, making sure that women play an inclusive and leading role in issues of business. Mine was to make sure I provide leadership and guidance so that is achieved. As part of my mandate inform of mentoring and couching, I've utilised these so as to achieve this dream. I am proud to know that I have invested most of my time in life trying to empower other people and over the years I did manage to produce the following:

- I produced a highly successful, socio economic and political conscious, responsible business woman
- Lindiwe Mtsweni was awarded the Best Young up and Coming Business Woman by the Local Government of eMalahleni
- Nkangala District Mayoral Special award for 2016 and 2017
- Recipient of the Top Business Woman of the year
- Community Development Programme award of the year from the Department of Culture Sport and Recreation 2015

I Malindi was mostly guided by our South African woman's chatter that gave me strength and direction to continue doing more than what was expected from me as a woman.

Just think about any business woman that you know and imagine if the woman's charter was not there would they make it? A big no!! Because the previous apartheid government made it a point that women feels inferior so that they do not even think of supporting their husbands during the struggle. Vitrovian is a black owned woman entity that aims to bring change to everyone from all walks of life

In 2014 I bought a building at Del Judor Street under Emalahleni municipality and named it Vitrovian House. It really makes me feel good to see myself owning such a huge building that accommodates a large number of people and other small business and companies who can rent space even though I was denied that opportunity to rent when I wanted to open Vitrovian in the first place.

After some few months Vitrovian started to employ more people from different communities and then started to stretch its wings as to touch more lives. New satellite/branch offices were opened in places such as Ogies (Phola) Bronkhorstspruit, Delmas, Emakhazeni and Middelburg while the head office is at Emalahleni, Vitrovian house in Del Judor. Vitrovian is the company that offers the following:

Consulting Services

VITROVIAN Trading and Projects (Pty) provides excellent, efficient and effective stakeholder management through community development and social facilitation, management consultancy, and sustainable development services to the private sector, parastatals and the public sector

Analytical Services

Vas Analytical Services offers commercial coal analytical services. Our state of the art laboratory complies with local and international standards i.e. ISO/IEC 17025: 2005 and SANAS. We are conveniently located within close proximity to the majority of mining houses in Delmas.

Vitromedia

VITROVIAN Media house was established in January 2016 for a reputation and innovative Media and Communication solutions that alter people's perceptions, transforms behaviour and builds lasting relationships with brands which informs consumer aspirations and inspires new behaviour.

Unothando foundation

Its foundation that targets mostly to non – Profit Organization, Faith based organizations, Community based organizations, Public benefit Trust, Section 21 Companies, Co- operatives and Youth Organizations, Civil Society Groups and Woman Organizations who do not have the capacity to source funds on their own but are doing a lot of work for the community. Unothando foundation is an umbrella body that has been seeking funds for all these organizations over the years and it will continue to do so for the benefit of our communities.

Unothando Foundation gave birth to Twinkle Little Sisters. Twinkle Little Sisters, which is about instilling and celebrating the spirit of excellence and hard work in young ladies. This initiative aims to teach young ladies that nothing great or sustainable is ever achieved in taking short cuts. This is especially important at this day and age where the "sugar daddy frenzy "and quick-fix mentality have blinded our young women.

Through this company, my new world of experience was born. Everything that I knew had to be added to the new experience of the corporate world. Most people who knew me back then were wondering as to how do I manage all this but the secret behind was love your neighbour as you love yourself, this simply means I would not do or achieve all this by myself but by the support of all my Vitrovian stuff members and the support of my community, based on the services that were rendered to them.

I am very proud with all the people around me because they all come to work knowing what is expected of them. They do their daily duties without being pushed. I strongly believe that our strategic plan of action from our employees which was introduced by our HR Nathi Nkomo has a lot to do with the energy behind our employees. We started some of our workers from zero to a high level; from being a floor cleaner to a receptionist and from being a receptionist to an office manager. We offer every individual an opportunity to further his/her studies whilst still working for the company. We groom, we empower and motivate our staff with all the skills required, as to boost the productivity level of **Vitrovian**.

I really wanted to make a difference without waiting for the government to keep promising change to our poor black people. I always choose to walk the talk and talk the walk. Looking back from where I started up to this far, I just feel so proud with what I have already accomplished in life.

Having a huge number of workers that are all working in my initiated businesses and my companies, serves the purpose of my existence. I learnt to understand that by giving one person a job you are unconsciously feeding 4 to 6 family members in one house within the community; therefore I will always strive to create more job opportunities for our people especially the youth. It really frustrates me to see young people who have spent most of their quality time in a tertiary institution but fail to get a job in return. For as long as I shall live I will fight this from all the corners of life and give a boost to our people.

The two projects which are close to my heart, because they give light and bring back hope to the youth of Nkangala (Take a girl child to work) in this project we as Vitrovian focus on local schools and select a group of girls to come and do practical office work based on their related careers and beyond. This project assist girls to choose a faculty that is best for them not what is best for their parents and friends. This is an annual project. Then there is Nkangala youth talent & sports development tournament.

Every committed and dedicated youth sports team that exist within Nkangala region are elected and then given an opportunity to come and participate in a sport tournament, this includes all the sporting codes in the district. We are proudly giving this opportunity to the youth because we came to believe that the wisdom of young people is in their energy. So we choose to empower them while they still have the energy to unleash their hidden talents and potential. As an office we spent our time meeting after meeting to organize for such big event that accommodates a large number of people in one place, people with common goal and common vision. The good results about this project are that it helps the youth to be part of drug free, teenage pregnancy free, alcohol free and crime free society. Above it all this company has donated food parcels and blankest to our poor black society and also provided a number of school kids with bursaries that were provided by Eskom (Kusile) power station, the number one Vitrovian supporting partner. I believe that Vitrovian will carry this through until every individual feels accommodated and equal within our communities.

Mphathiwezwe Nkabinde

As the manager at Medupi (Power station) for sustainability project I am always keen to see development in the economy of our people, being with Ms. Malindi in a business world has made us both to grow big and to have a healthy business relationship that is well maintained.

She's one person who conducts her business in a very professional manner. She always maintains discipline and adheres to business ethics. When I first met her at Kusile Power Station project while she was at Nkangala District in 2009 I then knew it that it is time for revolution, time for change, hard work and achievements.

You can't judge her presence in any business meetings or conference because she always speaks volume by giving a clear picture to everyone to see on what she's talking about. She is a spiritual, Social, Political and a very dedicated business person and she seem to know how to balance that very well. Her love for people is amazing.

Some people tend to forget their roots when they get their financial freedom. I have not seen that in her, she still talks about the same people she used to talk about years ago. That gives an indication that her circle of friends has not changed much. Her mother, child and the rest of the family is still her priority, and that is a sign of a much grounded person.

I wish most of the so called successful business people could behave the same after all the wealth that they have accumulated in life because with Ubuntu (humanity) you tend to win everyone's heart in the world. Malindi respect and fears God and I believe that it is the reason for her success, and I believe that her paths are guided from above to be as good and being humble as she is.

There was a point in my life where I felt Malindi was in to business because she is driven by the love of money, but when a person gives back to the community after making that money, then one starts to realize the difference between a selfish person and a go-getter.

She takes opportunities, at the same time she is very passionate about the environment she lives in. That is a character of a true leader, a leader that cares about her people. She is a true leader that allows others to lead her.

She served in politics and in government structures, when Malindi moved to business she allowed herself to be led by business leaders who have been in that field for years with their dynamic experiences of the cooperate world without allowing her ego or pride to stand on the way. She did not subject herself to trying to do things on her own and in her own way.

I believe that is what has enabled her to lead the business world today. She is a born leader, and those who have been led by her are proud of it, because of everyone who is from her leadership there is no doubt about it that he or she will be a product to his/her community.

The most amazing impact that I have learnt from her is that your background does not necessarily define your destiny. It is about telling yourself that now is the time to make a difference.

One can choose to cry over all missed opportunities, or decide to stay with what one is left with and try to change one's world. It is about knowing what can be changed, and put your energy in that.

What I like most about her is that she knows it for a fact that *life is 10% what happen to us and 90% how we react to it*. If there's anyone in the world who can ask me to predict Malindi's future, I will tell the world that whatever it is that she's looking forward to achieve she will get, because of the drive within her. One other thing is that she is gentle lion that survive in the jungle. My country must be proud to have produced such a magnificent leader like Malindi.

"A wise woman wishes to be no one's enemy; a wise woman refuses to be anyone's victim." Maya Angelou, 1928-2014

This is my short biography that tells more about my being (my Roots) and about what I have gone through to be this business woman that I am today

I Alphonsinah Lindiwe Mtsweni known as "Meme" born *on the 26th of August 1975.*

Sector 1: Member African National Congress:

1. African National Congress Youth League — Regional Secretary/ Provisional Member — 2000-2009

Sector 2: Local Government

1. Emalahleni Local Municipality — Councillor — 2000-2005
2. Nkangala District Municipality — Mayoral Committee Member — 2006-2010

Sector 3: Business
Business Knowledge

Vitrovian Trading and Projects (Pty) Ltd — Executive Chairwomen — 2011 to date

Sector	Sector knowledge	Experience
Community facilitation & Development	High	10 years
CIS Project & Enterprise Development	High	4 years
Management Consultant	High	4 years

Professional interests

Researching on emergency community liaison practices to offer leadership and insights into possible solutions for performance problems facing today's communities, businesses and individuals. Passionate about how community facilitation, learning and human performance improvement can be used to advance communities, business, drive profitability and reduce costs.

1. Established the company called Nonotsi that is dealing with cleaning services
2. Join the Nino's franchise
3. Also started a company called Vitrovian where I am an Executive Chairwoman that is doing Community Liaison, stakeholder management and social facilitation.
4. I also joined Rhapsody's group, open a shop (Bar Restaurant) at Witbank Benfluer Shopping Centre.
5. I recently open a commercial Coal Lab in Delmas.
6. And last but not list I started a Media company by the name of Vitromedia the brain child behind Vitrovian.
7. I have Unothando foundation that gave birth to Twinkle little sisters which is a girls only organisation.
8. I'm also the owner of a football club called Phola united FC and the Netball club that was lounged in 2015.
9. And I am also sponsoring the Industrial Robbers (bikers) from Phola/ Ogies who donates school uniforms, wheel chairs for physically challenged people & food parcels to the community annually.
10. In 2016 January I established Eyethu Wellness Centre that deals with Kidney Dialysis.

My view on community engagement and how business should support it

•   Every business affects and is also affected by the environment it operates from.

- For the business to be successful in achieving its objectives it must enhance the support of the community, it must manage threats which are imposed by the community.
- The community must be well informed about the status of the business, thus a constant communication must be maintained to get rid of the bad reputation about the business and create a favourable one, for the mutual benefit of the business.
- The business must try to win the support of the community by investing or ploughing back.
- There is no development without community.

What inspires me as a business person?

- Giving, because my community gave us life when our house was burnt into ashes.

One of the best things that I would like to do before I die.

- To open an educational trust for scholars.

    "To be really successful - and to have a settled sense of purpose that helps you finish projects - requires a clear understanding of the passion and skills you bring to the needs of your market." Finish What You Start.
    - Kerry Gene

    "Do not judge me by my successes,
    Judge me by how many times I
    Fell down and got back up again."
    - Nelson Mandela

That is how a successful business woman, an initiator, and helper in me was motivated, encouraged, developed and came to be.

Chapter 6

The Wisdom Behind Proper Coordination Of Staff Members

In my opinion I consider my staff members as my second family. These are the people who I spent most of my time with during week days. Staff members are like an engine of any existing business without them no business will run. I am always aware that the way I see them or classify them is not how they classify each other. One may think she/he is better than the others based on a position they occupy or on qualifications but to me all this does not make me treat them differently.

I believe that we are all born unique and every individual has a role to play. I always make sure that all my staff does understand the importance of cooperation. This has helped a lot in a sense that they now buy food during lunch and eat together as a family. This creates an opportunity to brainstorm about any challenge that an individual might be facing in his position (work related challenges or social challenges).

It becomes more of being family members rather than just being colleagues. I choose not to under estimate the worth of another human being because you will never know who will save your live along the line. As I am stating this I remember Ms. Thembi Bokondo who was the Stability & stakeholder manager in my company. This woman made me realize that there are times in life where you cannot carry a load by yourself any more but others will carry it for you. Lucy Mtsweni my mother was very sick, I did whatever I could to save her life.

I tried every hospital and Doctors I knew until I became powerless. Thembi took me by surprise when she came to my mother's place and said this time we need no one else to rely on but God. I didn't question her because I knew what she was saying was nothing but the truth. So we both knelt down and started to pray very hard until I was in tears.

I used to consider myself as a very strong woman but when it came to a point of seeing my mother's life ending in front of me I just felt so weak. After a long prayer, we took her to hospital once again and spent the whole night there waiting for the results from the Doctor.

When they say through prayer there is a light surely there is, after spending the whole night at the hospital the Doctor came and us the positive news about the status of my mother that she is now at the state of recovering better than before. Through it all I was not with my biological sister nor my friend nor my relative but one of my staff members. This type of support was given back to me because of the total love that I have for my staff members.

It is true that what you put in is what you will get out. Today my mother's life was saved by someone I did not think will be. This is a lesson to us as entrepreneurs or leaders to know that when one starts a business you need to always be aware of how you treat your employees.

Do not be like most leaders who push too hard to be recognized, just take a look at all the leaders that you know on earth that were ruling with the autocratic system or monarch system as to where they are they today. They usually don't make it; due to the fact that they put themselves first and their people last.

The whole country becomes affected because of one's ego. This also happen in our homes, where fathers are like lions. They are feared. They want their presence felt. Well they will oblige the first time, the second time but the third time kids will have a better way of handling or dealing with the situation. Every time when he comes through the door, every child pretend to be busy for instance pretending to be studying, watching TV or any house chores and this is how they will avoid him and as a result they will shut him out of their world, they will isolate him and no relations will be built. They will give you what you prefer not what they prefer. Employees will also behave like that.

At the end of the year you will be expecting nothing but positive results from their school reports with confidence because they were studying hard throughout the year and the results speaks the opposite because they never studied all they did was to pretend. So the same applies to our employees. Do not run after them let them run the race by themselves, do not be too hard to them, do not be pushy just monitor and advice.

Make them to enjoy the benefits the company offers based on their best service they deliver and productivity. At the end of the year celebrate with them and have a party with them so that they can do more the following year.

I am humbled by the fact that I have been travelling around the world so as to form partnerships with other entrepreneurs but I never panicked as to what I will find when I come back home because my company will run even when I am not there. I want it to run even when I am no more. I am saying this because I believe in the seed that I have planted in all of my staff members.

Don't let your team wonder if they're on the right track make them to know!!!

There are a number of educational books that teaches more about staff coordination (staff management). I also do recommend them because the teachings are genuine. My mother could not stop feeling grateful because of the people who would come to her just to say thank you for giving birth to such a humble person because today they can put food on their tables for their families because of all the job opportunities that I created for them. I can have all the money in the world and all the luxury assets but if I fail to give life to the next person I just feel worthless.

Sibongile Shongwe my old time family friend once taught me that never look down to those old Aunties and Uncles that are known as alcoholics within your community because as black people this happen to be the people who will give the last tribute by giving a helping hand during the preparation of your funeral, from day one till the last day when you go six feet underground.

They give their time and their efforts to support the family even though they won't be in a position to assist with money but their hands does everything in support of the family that is in mourning. So never characterise people with their defects of characters. With all the knowledge shared on this book I'm humbly doing so as to empower other woman who wishes to follow in my foot steps and achieve the best in life. Just have more than what I have, achieve more than what I have already achieved, built a business empire that is triple bigger and lager than Vitrovian and don't forget to double the number of my employees 5 times annually. Please make that change because you can.

Start that business, start that company, wait for no one, just do it. There is no right time or right moment to do things in life we create the right moments in life. Words of advice; every time you select your staff for your business just bear in mind that not everyone has to have diplomas and degrease because your staff are like a soccer club, every player has a role on the team. Allow them to show you what they can do on the pitch rather than what their profiles can proclaim about them.

Emmanuel Mashego (KG) tells more about the dynamic impact and the influence of Malindi to people from all different walks of life.

"No matter what life has thrown at you, you're the master of your destination"

Malindi, as she is internationally known is a born astonishing leader who some of us have met on many platforms. However two things stands out, one being the former but lifetime secretary of the ANC Youth League in the Nkangala Region, the first women for that matter, who led with distinction, resilience and selflessness.

Her leadership credential and foresight surpasses many women leadership of her life time because of her potential to spot opportunities and talents within individuals, which many leaders of today are failing to grasp. That a true leader sees talent in an individual as an opportunity to nurture as opposed to opposition and competition.

The second attribute, comes from the highly successful business women, who in a short space of time was able to achieve dreams made of lifetime successes and/or achievements. She holds the empowerment of women close to her heart and is a living champion of those interests, as seen with the many women who occupy leadership roles in businesses she's got interests in.

One cannot over emphasize her "Philanthropic" work that she is involved in. Community work is what keeps her sane, for a lack of a better term. One would have to write a separate book about her work thus far.

"You have set the mark; I hope other young women and men alike are ready to take the baton and make the difference they so desire". Respect ... General!!!

> "The two most important
> Days in your life are the day you are born,
> And the day you find out why."
> - Mark Twain

That is how a grateful woman, an empowerment, and an opportunity creator in me was motivated, encouraged, developed and came to be.

Chapter 7

Sa Woman With The Ability
To Run Their Own Race

I believe that success is your birth right so go out there and claim it because it is yours.

An apple does not fall far from its tree, so what kind of a fruit are you? And from which tree did you fall? Are you a bitter fruit or a sweet fruit?

In your list you have a number of people that grew up with you, who are more successful in life. Don't you want to know how they did it? Don't be ignorant, research and follow on their footsteps because it is never too late to make that change in your life.

What matters most in life is not how other people perceive you but how you perceive yourself, if you stand in front of a mirror and see a cat standing there then you have a problem because you are not a cat but a lion, king of the jungle so allow that sleeping giant of a lion to arise and roar!!! You must make women count as much as men; you must have an equal standard of morals; and the only way to enforce that is through giving women political power so that you can get that equal moral standard registered in the laws of the country. It is the only way.

I am a woman so I talk more about what I have noted in my world about the magnificent role women has played so far to protect and to change the world. You don't have to like this but it is an inescapable fact that women have done so much to protect this planet called earth.

Do you still remember Hiroshima? In August 1945, during the final stage of the Second World War, the United States dropped atomic bomb on the Japanese cities of Hiroshima and Nagasaki. The two bombings, which killed at least 129,000 people, remain the only use of nuclear weapons for warfare in history, after the war woman who survived had to pick up the pieces and rebuilt the country.

Women always pickup pieces after losing everything that belongs to them and their families and husbands that were killed on a battle field but God has given women courage.

Women are able to carry all the baggage of sorrows, pains, tears, trauma and still stand tall to re-unite the nation. Prayer ceremonies are initiated because that is the first step of re-uniting the broken nation.

Seeking for any available food for others to eat is their role too. In all the wars in this world women are the most vulnerable and mostly affected by the after effects of the war. Women are not quick to say this is the end of the world rather they are too quick to say what will happen after this storm. They are visionary. They are more concerned about the future more than today. It is inborn for woman to always be concern about the future, look at the pregnant woman; she worries most about the future of the child not about the pains of giving birth to the child.

I have discovered that majority of NGO's and Community projects are initiated and implemented by women. This implies that women are concerned about things that affect the society, such as unemployment; drug abuse; the HIV and AIDS; crime; and poverty among others.

Women will sit around the table in a board meeting to find solutions to the challenges and problems.

Orphans and abandoned children are a responsibility of government however government is not pulling its weight instead its women who run around day in and day out like headless chickens to find sponsors. They do all this to find money and food parcels for the Orphans and abandoned children to survive with or without government contributions.

These women always make sure that all those Orphans and abandoned children get food to eat on daily basis. The magical part about this kind of a vision is that it is not based on manipulating any government system but on giving life to the lifeless, hope to the hopeless and a better life for all. Just to prove my statement take a look at how many women are street vendors especially in South Africa, they push so hard just to make a difference.

Nobody is pushing them to do so but unemployment rate and poverty. There is no one who can take away that power they possess because it is an inborn thing. It is a God-given potential. Behind every successful woman there is hard work. *#Malibongwe Igama Lamakhosikazi.*

My mother Lucy once told me that back then when they were still close with my father they had a fight and through this fight my father decided to move her out of the house including myself and my siblings. She had nowhere to go, she then took us with her to her workplace where she was working as a domestic worker and her employers were white people. She had to relate the whole story to them as to what brought us there.

The main thing was to be accommodated not just for a night but 2 to 4 months. Remember the country was still under apartheid system, so for a white family to keep in a black person in his/her house was against the law but her employers decided to violate that law by accommodating us.

Every afternoon when we were coming back from school we were collected by my mother's employer, she knew that it was a high risk to keep us under her roof but she took that risk and sacrificed her life for our lives. This became an eye opener to me as I grew older that not all white people during the apartheid time were bad.

The system made everyone to wear a mask so as to save his/her skin, meaning it was not easy to reveal your true identity because of the racial segregation. It was not easy for an individual to be himself and show how kind and caring they were. There was a thin line between love and hate. I'm still humbled to know that there were a number of white people who did their best to help our black people back then.

**"Develop an attitude of gratitude
Say thank you to everyone
You meet for everything
They do for you".**

Life is like a roller coaster because at one minute you are up the next minute you are down. No one deserves a bitter life. We all want what is best for our lives. The moment you realize that you have lost everything you have that's when your mind starts to unlock itself, helping you to think until you find a solution to what you are facing. Be proud of being part South African women and don't even forget our roots.

Do not be part of any xenophobic attacks that is created by the mob justice because some of our leaders and our relatives were given a better place to stay by foreign countries during apartheid government. Let the spirit of Ubuntu continue to live in you. Blacks against blacks and white against any nation, this must come to an end.

Leaving a positive legacy behind with no blood in our hands is what is expected of us. There are a number of women who chose to do well in my country and I will always pay respect to their magnificent efforts to be where they are today.

The likes of Noni Gasa the fashion designer, Uyanda Mbuli Diamond Face Couture Pty Ltd, not forgetting the Stone Cherry lady Ms. Khensani Mangayi-Nkosi These women are brand managers, this goes to prove to many South Africans that "the vision you glorify in your mind, the ideal you enthrone in your heart this you will build your life by, this you will become".

They started from the ground to be where they are today. Really South Africa is alive with possibilities, don't you still notice that? Just wake up and smell the coffee because you can achieve too. You are not different from these women mentioned above; you can still rise against all odds.

So you too can win. As a woman, learn to take each day as it comes don't rush it. You are greater than what you think you are, you just have to realize that before the sun goes down. Many people from our neighbouring countries wish they were South African citizens, so to utilize all the rich opportunities that South Africa has.

You are a South African woman but doing nothing about these rich opportunities around you. Life is there to offer you anything that you think belongs to you. Stand for it, fight for it and claim it.

Remember you need to be in tune with yourself. Discipline yourself; walk tall even though at times you are faced with some defect of character in your life but still just walk tall.

Remember you are a woman so keep your dignity and shape that character and make this world a better place for all of us to live in. Let us take a look at the following profiles of the best woman who inspires me the most in life.

Remember learn more about others as to grow more from where you are.

Santie Botha

Santie Botha is chancellor of the Nelson Mandela Metropolitan University in Port Elizabeth – at 48, the youngest chancellor in South Africa and serves on the board of Tiger Brands Limited and Famous Brands. She is a South African marketing pioneer who played a role in the success of the 2010 World Cup as head of marketing at FIFA sponsor MTN.

Botha joined MTN as chief marketing officer in 2003 and soon made a splash when she painted OR Tambo Airport yellow (the brand's signature colour). During her time at MTN, she helped embed the brand in Africa and the Middle East. But her main legacy was that a company born in Africa became the first ever global sponsor of the FIFA World Cup.

Botha has won a number of awards, including the 2010 Business woman of the Year award from the Businesswomen's Association of

South Africa, Marketer of the Year in 2002, The Star Top 10 Business people in South Africa 2003 and Young Business Person of the Year in 1998.

Botha is one of South Africa's top 10 wealthiest women.

The role of a chancellor is traditionally that of a figurehead, but Botha has said she plans to play an active role in developing the institution as a place of learning and as a brand.

If you want to see real development in the world then our best investment is in WOMEN." - Desmond TUTU

Testimony by Cherilee Allay

My Boss is a true Leader; where do I start telling the world about her because I have so many things to say, but one thing for sure my Boss Ms. Mtsweni is a true leader and has a huge impact on my career not just only at work but everywhere in my life, she is the role model in my life that inspires me to dream more, learn more, think more and do much more than what I could have ever imagined.

Ms. Mtsweni is very humble, strong and sweet person that is always there when you need her to be, we at Vitrovian are very fortunate to have someone like Ms. Mtsweni in and around us to mould us in becoming something we have been dreaming of becoming in life.

She always makes me feel that I can take on the world when everything from my side is not going well; she is one person who believes in me and understands me. She makes me take steps to the next level, she is there to help me grow and become someone in life instead of sitting on the doorstep the rest of my life. She has shown me what life is all about, and I thank her from the bottom of my heart, she is the one person who guided me through my life's journey and is still doing so.

When I started at Vitrovian I was an ordinary receptionist for about a year. As time went by she saw something in me which no one saw. She promoted me to work in Finance and her Personal assistant, today I stand tall to say that I run the office and I am the Office Manager that keeps things going and running smoothly, all because of her giving me a chance in life.

I want to say thank you Ms. Mtsweni for guiding me through life and still doing what she does best to push me to the limit. She helped me grow from strength to strength and made me the person I am today, without her in my life who knows where I could have been? It is people like her that inspired me to take a step further when it all seemed impossible.

"Malindi you are a true blessing in my life and I appreciate all the ropes that you taught me both in life and in business, my career today is on the upward way it is all because you believing in me, you are the one person who gave me a chance in life! You are really an inspiration not just to me but to a lot of other people as well."

Being a white lady in black dominated work place has made me realize that all the freedom fighters that died along the line for the liberation of this country, their main objective was for us to enjoy this democratic life style or culture that I'm enjoying today. Every time when I have to give my blankets a kick and go to work I do so willingly because of the warm and welcoming environment at my work place irrespective of the difference of the colour of my skin, different languages and race. Unity is what keeps us moving together in the same direction to achieve more.

Women's Lot:

As women we share with our menfolk the cares and anxieties imposed by poverty and its evils. As wives and mothers, it falls upon us to make small wages stretch a long way. It is we who feel the cries of our children when they are hungry and sick. It is our lot to keep and care for the homes that are too small, broken and dirty to be kept clean. We know the burden of looking after children and land when our husbands are away in the mines, on the farms, and in the towns earning our daily bread.

We know what it is to keep family life going in pondokkies and shanties, or in overcrowded one-room apartments. We know the bitterness of children taken to lawless ways, or daughters becoming unmarried mothers whilst still at school, or boys and girls growing up without education, training or jobs at a living wage.

Equality for Women:

We resolve to struggle for the removal of laws and customs that deny African women the right to own, or inherit property. We resolve to work for a change in the laws of marriage such as are found amongst our African, Malay and Indian people, which has the effect of placing wives in the position of legal subjection to husbands, and giving husbands the power to dispose of wives' property and earnings, and dictate to them in all matters affecting them and their children.

All that is written from our Freedom charter and from our Woman's charter it really proves to the world that as South Africans we really knew what we wanted. We needed more than what money could buy; freedom and a better life to the next generation.

I believe in capacitating myself, these are the readings that contributed in making me who I am today.

- The Women's Charter
- Trade unionism blossoms and women become more assertive, 1930s
- UDF Women's Congress
- Women at the start of the 20th century
- Women in the new democracy
- Women in the schizophrenic 1940s - World War II and its aftermath
- Women protection and representation in South Africa after 20 years of democracy
- Women, employment and the changing economic scene, 1920s
- Women's Enfranchisement Association of the Union (WEAU)
- Women's liberation by Zanele Dhlamini (Mbeki)
- Women's March Interviews
- Women's National Coalition

A Single Society:

We women do not form a society separate from the men. There is only one society, and it is made up of both women and men. As women we share the problems and anxieties of our men, and join hands with them to remove social evils and obstacles so as to progress.

Poor and Rich:

These are evils that need not exist. They exist because the society in which we live is divided into poor and rich, into black and white. They exist because there are privileges for the few, discrimination and harsh treatment for the many. We women have stood and will stand shoulder to shoulder with our menfolk in a common struggle against poverty, race and class discrimination, and the evils of the colour bar.

Test of Civilisation:

The level of civilization which any society has reached can be measured by the degree of freedom that its members enjoy. The status of women is a test of civilization. Measured by that standard, South Africa must be considered low in the scale of civilized nations.

"If you can't fly, then run,
if you can't run, then walk,
if you can't walk, then crawl,
but whatever you do,
you have to keep moving forward."
– Martin Luther King Jr.

That is how a strong woman, a woman of strength, and a woman mentor in me was motivated, encouraged, developed and came to be.

Chapter 8

Lucky Ndinisa The Political Brain Engine Behind Malindi

The real motive behind my involvement in political world was the freedom charter. It gave us hope when we were in darkens about the future of this country. That is why I dedicated my life to the African national congress. This was not based on self-interest but for the liberation of our black society even though in today's life you will find most of our political leaders misusing the opportunities which are brought by the liberation and charter.

I was too involved in politics in a sense that I have spent my quality time while I was at university attending libraries reading books that could help me see the world in colours rather than to see the world in black and white.

National Liberation:

As members of the National Liberation Movement and Trade Unions, in and through our various organisations, we march forward with our men in the struggle for liberation and the defence of the working people. We pledge ourselves to keep the banner of equality, fraternity and liberty high. As women there rests upon us also the burden of removing from our society all the social differences as a result of the past between men and women, which have the effect of keeping our sex in a position of inferiority and subordination.

When I was a regional secretary for ANCYL in Nkangala I worked with Linah Malatjie. Linah became a sister to me, she groomed me, and she taught me lots of things about life. Our relationship became so strong such that I started to regard her as my mother. She played a significant role in my life, she was my mentor.

Our wish was to build the strong ANC and make it grows big and to be where it is now even though the two of us we were affected by the developments that were taking place within the ANC but we stood together and supported each through all the adversities of life.

Lucky Ndinisa has been with me in almost all of the ANC offices and conferences.

As he attests: "I am humble to know that Malindi regards me as an influence in her political career.

I was only doing what I do best, and am still doing it to and for others, it only depends on an individual, whether you implement my teachings or ignore them. I feel so proud to see her being the person she has become, a solution to our social economic problems. I real can't proclaim the honour of being the master mind behind Malindi's success.

OH!!! Yes one may say I'm the one who groomed her but I personally say I just added some few drops of water over her already overflowing cup of knowledge because she was at the right place, in the right political party at the right time. I did not recruit Malindi in the ANC structures I found her there. The first time we actually met was at the regional conference while I was elected as the regional secretary of the youth league for Witbank region and I was from a small town called Watervalboven (Emakhazeni) and she was also a youth league member.

She was also from a small town named Phola/Ogies. We were both coming from deferent places but when it came to our call of duty no matter how far we were meeting, Malindi was always punctual. Considering that in those years we had no cars for the organization so we had to make it on time no matter what.

The African National Congress Youth League (ANCYL) office at that time had no deputies; we only had the chair person, secretary and the treasurer with additional members. She was elected as an additional member in that meeting. I was the Regional Secretary; it was a very difficult position to hold because the secretary is the engine of the Organization. This simply meant if the organization is doing well it becomes a collective work but if the organization is not doing well then everyone will point fingers and put the blame on the secretary that he is not doing his work. So as I continue with my day by day work I then came to notice that this position needs a deputy secretary. Along the line in one of our meetings I then requested that our office should have a deputy secretary so as to minimize the heavy load of the secretary. We had to discuss it over and over again up until my wish was granted and the committee decided to elect Malindi (Meme) as the deputy secretary of the Youth League. Culture makes people understand each other better. And if they understand each other better in their soul, it is easier to overcome the economic and political barriers.

Meme then took over and started assisting me with all the administration work within the office, making sure that the organization is stable and is running properly. She was very dedicated and very professional in her work for a period of 18 months. When we merged the Western region with the Witbank region we were then called Nkangala region. The leadership debate started because we were now merging two separate structures. Once again Malindi was elected as the regional secretary of Nkangala region based on her hard work, commitment and for being loyal to the organization.

"Good, better, best.
Never let it rest.
Till your good is better and your better is best.
- St. Jerome.

The best word to describe Malindi within the organization was, Gogo meaning the grandmother of the organization because she was promoted from one office to another office moving side by side with me, gaining more experience than ever.

She was a very talkative person, creative and very problematic at times especially when things needed to be pushed; she was not just putting her efforts but putting her massive efforts for a job well done within the organization.

Meme had a dream about her community. She wanted what was best for the people. When she ventured into business sector, I then knew in my heart that she's going to make it due to the strong foundation that her career was built on. She was moulded by the best revolutionist of the ANC in our offices. Looking at her success today I just feel so proud because she's now what we all wanted her to be, a product for the people. It is true that crops do not get harvested were seeds were not planted, so Meme was the right seed to a fertile soil and that is why we are all enjoying the fruits of her success today.

> "The truth is, when you have little to do, you do very
> little. But when you have much to do, you do much.
> So it should make sense that by taking on more than
> you can handle, you accomplish more than you ever
> dreamed you could. And so it is."
> — Richelle E. Goodrich.

I ended up being less active from the party because I felt like we have lost our major focus and have directed all our efforts in fighting each other within the same organization. All the promises that were made to our society were now nowhere on the agenda. I am not to saying the ANC never accomplished some of the things that they promised. No!!! They really did but the internal fights really do cause damage to the party. Every time when they want to remove you from the party especially when you are a woman you become a soft target the movement need to enforce woman emancipation program to be actively up and running at all the levels within the country.

If this system can be properly implemented then the opposition parties will have nothing to capitalize on. This might also bring back the dignity of the ANC. Internal fights has made most ANC followers to give up on the party and this needs to be fixed one way or another.

Clearance Maseko AKA **Bafo** share his testimony about Malindi.

I have been working from a distance with this woman before I came close and work under her kingdom. What I noted about Malindi is that she is nothing but a revolutionist, a social activist, a distinguish commander of note, a true combatant, a leader and an entrepreneur.

I personally consider her as a visionary person because she sees beyond limits. When she starts a race she always makes it a point that she runs until the finish line. I strongly believe that if Malindi was born earlier, around 50s and 60s she was going to join the Umkhonto Wesizwe (Mk). I'm saying this because I have notice the patriotic spirit that lives within her. Fighting and sacrificing her life for the lives of others and even die in the battle field that is what she is all about.

She was born for this course. She has been involved in numerous ANC projects and offices. She was elected as the first female secretary general of the African national Congress Youth League (ANCYL) in Nkangala Region

> ➤ The ex-officio (PEC) member of the youth league in Mpumalanga.
> ➤ The ex-officio (ANC REC) member & member of (RWC)
> ➤ A Convenor/Scriber (RTT) of the Youth League in Nkangala.
> ➤ The Cllr (PR) Emalahleni municipality
> ➤ MMC-Social development. (member of the mayoral committee) at Nkangala District Municipality.

Malindi is one people who will represent us better in parliament one day. I believe that one day she will be forced back to the ANC offices by popular demand because of her organic intelligence that she purses from within for the movement.

Just read the freedom charter and evaluate the aims and objectives of the charter and compare it with the strategic plan of the African

Chapter 9

Let The Bygones Be Bygones

Looking back to what South Africa was and the way it is today it real makes me feel more inspired with change. Indeed everything is temporary but change is permanent. Wiseman usually says the richest place in the world is the graveyards no wonder why they say so. If you look at my life on how I was raised one can simply tell that I had no promising future and if I allowed my background to rule over me and suddenly died along the way then my potential and my wisdom could have perished into the grave. By choosing to fight back all the challenges I had back then today more lives are saved by my existence.

My Mother Lucy when I ask her what is it that I can do for her whilst still live? She's quickly answered me by saying you have already done everything for me. "You even exceeded my expectations to a point where you even closed the void within me of raising you all as a single parent, even if I can die now I will just rest in peace knowing that I have left you behind to take care of everyone." My mom found it so difficult to understand the inner me, the quiet and humble soul that I am.

Our relatives from my father's side have never been there for us when we needed them the most and my father as well, but trust me today if there is anything they need I give them with an open heart, if anyone dies I always choose to spend as much as I can just to make sure that he or she get a proper and a dignified funeral. I strongly believe that by letting bygones be bygones you are automatically setting your soul free from the past and focus more on the future.

You cannot really move forward whilst you are still holding on to the past, sometimes you just need to throw your mind, your soul and your heart into the future then your body will automatically follow. Just let the past be where they belong, in the past!

Some people really do not know on how special it feels to know that you have a number of scholars who are at universities because of the leadership and bursaries that you have given out every year and families who sleeps daily having food in their stomach because of your contribution. You may even ask the likes of Oprah Winfrey as to how special it feels like after establishing a Leadership Academy for Girls in South Africa so as to give a quality education by investing in young girls.

If you have too much food on your plate please share it with others. Remember God always give more to those who share what they have with others.

> "When a poor person dies of hunger, it has
> not happened because God did not take care
> of him or her. It has happened because either
> you or I failed to give that person what he
> or she needed."

Most people who have made it in life come from nothing to something. The great inventors were regarded as nobodies until they achieved their dreams and become some- bodies. We are what we are because of what we are repeatedly doing with excellence it is no-longer not an act but a habit. For ones dream to become a reality it needs a total believe with massive efforts.

> "Life's battles do not always go to the stronger or the faster man
> but to those who thinks they can win". by Walt Disney

- Walt Disney was employed as a driver of an ambulance for Red Cross but today his known as the creator of Micky Mouse.
- A graduate who struggled to get a permanent job became A professor and an inventor with his most popular equation E=MC2. That's Albert Einstein.
- A neglected child became an icon. That's Oprah Winfrey
- A programmer became the richest man. That's Bill Gate
- The woman who worked in cafes wrote Harry Potter. That's JR Rowling.
- The man who was defeated 8 times in elections but finally became the greatest president ever. That's Abraham Lincoln.

These were just ordinary people, just like you and I until they started believing in their dreams. So who are you not to be? Remember we are all living in borrowed times; we are not going to stay forever in this world. So live your dream while you still can!

Yes there will be times when you feel like you are just walking in the desert with no trees to provide you with oxygen and no rivers to drink water from, do not stop, keep moving forward because at the end of the desert the green grass start to grow. Accept to lose some other battles in your life and put your energy and your focus on winning a war that is within you. This means you vs. yourself.

"Don't watch the clock; do what the clock does
By moving forward!! Clock wise not
Anti-clock wise; till your dreams are met!

That is how a forgiving being, a family binder, and a graceful being in me was motivated, encouraged, developed and came to be.

MY MOM'S OBITUARY

Lucy Nozimango Dimakatso Majodina was born 1952-05-18 in Jagersfontein a small village in the Free State province. She spent her childhood years in Koffiefontein where she attended school at Bantu Community School, achieving Standard 6 "Royal Reading".

She was fondly named Dimakatso by her father John and late mother Khaketso Majodina. She was the second born form 8 siblings (4 sisters and 4 brothers).

In 1970 she gave birth to her late son King and in 1972 gave birth to her late daughter Manko. In 1974 she met her late husband Zephinia Mtsweni in Koffiefontein whom the family fondly called Kontrak. Together they moved to Ogies where she gave birth to her daughter Lindiwe known as Meme.

In 1979 she gave birth to her son Bhuti, her daughter Vuyiswa in 1982 and the last born son Bafana in 1986. She left behind her 3 sisters, 2 brothers, 4 children (two boys and two girls) and 11 grandchildren.

To fulfill her spiritual life and her walk with Christ, Mme Dimakatso was a member of the LGV prophetic church that is now known as the Light House where she served as an Elder of the church.

POLITICAL LIFE

During the 80s and 90s she actively participated in Civic organizations that fought for human rights and community development focused on Land occupations. This led to the establishment of Evezi and Oyco human settlement under the leadership of Kenneth Ngcongwane and Bishop Jacobs.

In the 90s and 2000s she was an activist member of the ANC Woman's League in the then Highveld region which included Phola, Witbank, Kriel, Rietspruit and some mining areas. This political involvement continued in the Phola/Ogies Branch up to her passing.

Further she distinguished herself as a leader of SANCO at Phola Ogies under the leadership of the late Mr. Thomas Sindane.

Some of her memorable moments in political life, was when she actively participated in the important realignment process of the ANC inside the country, which led to amongst others the renaming of Nkangala as region and Mpumalanga province.

True to her commitment to the struggle for liberation, Mme Dimakatso was nominated to form part of ANC delegation to its 1997 National Conference in Mafikeng.

Mme Dimakatso Majodina demonstrated her special talents, attributes and skills as a brave strategist and selfless cadre of the movement.

In the community (ward 31), she served as a member of the Ward Committee from 2004 – 2010; the School Governing Body (SGB) at Mehlwana Secondary School, contributing quite significantly to the promotion of education.

She met her untimely death still serving as a member of the ANC Veteran's League in the Nkangala Region and as a fiery community leader.

[Lala Ngoxolo (Rest in eternal peace.........)

Chapter 10
Gallery

MALINDI DURING THE ANC MOMENTUM

MY DAUGHTER ZINHLE

GIVING BACK TO THE COMMUNITY AND ALSO INVESTING TO THE YOUTH

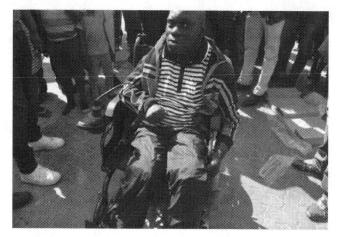

EMBRACING MY NDEBELE CULTURE

MALINDI (I RUN MY OWN RACE)

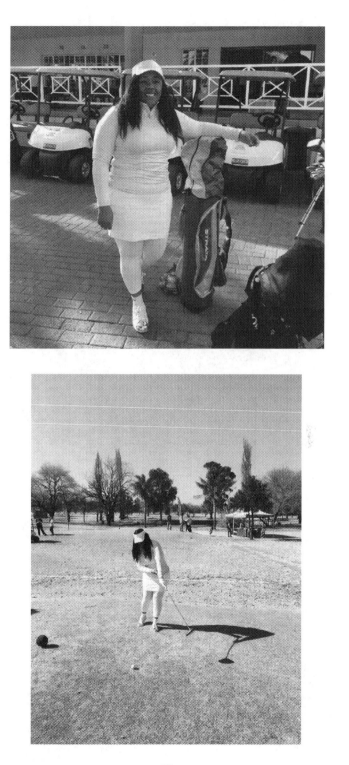

NKANGALA YOUTH TALENT AND SPORTS DEVELOPMENT TOURNAMENT

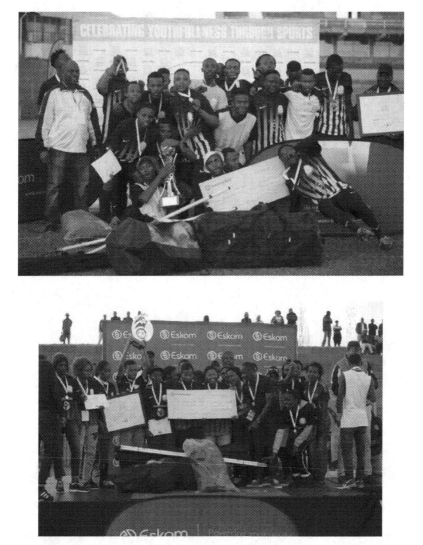

SILECTING THE RIGTH STUFF FOR A JOB WELL DONE AND SHARE THE LOVE WITH EVERYONE YOU MEET!!!

A LONG JOURNEY WALKED

WITH GROWTH, LESSONS AND ACHIEMENTS!!!

Printed in the United States
By Bookmasters